NEW EN

CONTENTS

Published by Gallery Books
A Division of W H Smith Publishers Inc.
112 Madison Avenue
New York, New York 10016

Produced by
Bison Books Corp.
15 Sherwood Place
Greenwich, CT 06830

ISBN 0-8317-6320-5

Printed in Hong Kong

2 3 4 5 6 7 8 9 10

GLAND

TEXT   BARBARA PAULDING THRASHER

DESIGN   MIKE ROSE

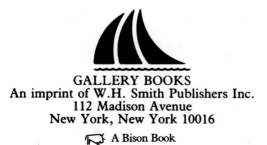

GALLERY BOOKS
An imprint of W.H. Smith Publishers Inc.
112 Madison Avenue
New York, New York 10016

A Bison Book

For Jeff

Photo credits

Bob Baldridge: 54-55
Marcello Bertinetti: 1, 37, 40, 41, 52, 86, 87, 94, 100,
  103, 107, 114-15
Jeff Blechman: 56, 116, 126
Tim Finnemore, First Aroostook Corp., Caribou, Maine:
  62-63
John Foraste/Brown University: 112, 113, 120
FPG International: J Blank (31, 38-39, 91, 95);
M Brooke (101); J F Buchholz (61); F Dole (78-79);
Fujsaki (96); F Grehan (59, 60, 68-69); N Groffman (24-25);
J Hailey (53); D Hallinan (16-17); J Pearson (110-11);
J Randkleu (32); C H Smith (64, 72, 74-75); J Viesti (121);
W Wilson (30)
Jeff Gnass: 3-6, 15, 27, 33, 34-35, 48, 49, 57, 82-83
H Armstrong Roberts: 18, 22, 26, 28-29, 42, 50-51, 84-85;
P Avis (23); J Gleiter (118-19); A Griffin (20-21, 44-45);
R Krubner (19); F Sieb (76, 77); J Spratt (46-47);
D Winston (66)
John Katsigianis: 65, 123, 124-25
Douglas K Paulding: 70-71
Jerry Sieve: 67, 73, 104-05
Mike Tamborrino: 97, 106, 122
Barbara Paulding Thrasher: 43
Vermont Travel Division: 108-09
Angela White: 80, 88-89, 90, 98, 99, 117

INTRODUCTION

New England! The very name evokes images of rolling hills bathed in the scarlets and yellows of autumn, narrow roads banked by towering snowdrifts, lighthouses blinking their warnings across dark waters, seashell collectors roaming sandy beaches while children play in the surf, clear mountain streams working their way through a wilderness forest, brightly colored skiers snaking through mogul fields, and rustic country stores. But underlying all these impressions of New England is a heritage that gives unity to the region, pride to its inhabitants, and fascination to its many visitors.

The region that is New England—comprising six states—covers 66,608 square miles of America's extreme Northeast. Aptly dubbed 'the birthplace of America,' New England has a history that antedates the white man's arrival by thousands of years. The oldest evidence of human life, discovered in Vermont, dates back to approximately 9000 BC and indicates a people of Mongolian descent whose path can be traced westward all the way across America and beyond. Apparently they crossed over the Bering land bridge from Asia millennia ago. Although some believe the area was visited and briefly settled by Vikings about AD 1000, others deny the possibility. By the time Christopher Columbus and subsequent fortune hunters landed on America's eastern shore, 25,000 Algonquian Indians lived in New England—Indians who would help the Pilgrims from Plymouth, England, weather their first winter in Plymouth, Massachusetts in 1621.

Within a decade many more would emigrate to this new world, settling first in Massachusetts, then in Maine and Connecticut. Although their religious beliefs had brought them persecution in England, the Puritans became equally, if not more, intolerant of those who believed differently from themselves than their oppressors had been. The Reverend Roger Williams, banned for his liberal teachings, established a settlement on land granted by the Indians, which would become the city of Providence in an area which his maligners dubbed 'Rogue's Island.' As the white population increased, the Indians were dispossessed and pressed into conformity. When they resisted, many were killed in skirmishes, culminating in the carnage of King Philip's War (1675-76).

New England is dotted with statues and historic places that tell the well-known story of America's fight for independence, beginning with the first clash between the Minutemen and the British Army in 1775 in Lexington, north of Boston, and ending six years later. Her integrity as a nation intact, America then turned to industrial and cultural development and commerce. In this, too, New England was the leader. A tenuous maritime economy gave way to a growing textile industry, as men and women left the farms to work the factories and mills. Schools and museums flourished, as did the arts.

However, despite the region's continuing literary tradition and the proliferation of educational institutions, and despite New England's pre-eminence as a leader in abolitionism and social reform, after the Civil War its status began to decline. As industry moved south to take advantage of cheaper labor and more available resources, political corruption and disintegration accompanied the struggling economy and the disparate forces brought by waves of immigration. Cultural suppression became an attempt to restore the spirit of New England, which reached an all-time low as the area was hit hard by the Great Depression. But New England emerged from her troubles strengthened and ready to play a role in modern America. A changed and renewed industry based on high technology, insurance, and tourism accompanied political revival. Mills and factories, closed for decades, have been renovated and reopened as offices, housing complexes, warehouses and marketplaces. From Maine to Connecticut, ethnic diversity has lent depth to New England's character.

New England would nurture such writers as Henry David Thoreau, Ralph Waldo Emerson, Nathaniel Hawthorne, Harriet Beecher Stowe, Henry Wadsworth Longfellow, Herman Melville, Robert Lowell, Emily Dickinson, Wallace Stevens and the quintessential New England poet, Robert Frost.

New England, more than a history, is also a landscape—a mosaic of geological features. Its mountains tell of the land's violent upheavals two billion years ago. Its rockbound coast bespeaks the glacial retreat that succeeded the Ice Age some 11,000 years ago. New England's mountains are part of the Appalachian system, stretching from the Berkshires in western Massachusetts northeast through Vermont, as the Green Mountains, through New Hampshire, as the White Mountains, and into Maine as the Mahoosuc Range. For anyone who has ever viewed New Hampshire's Franconia Notch from the lofty peak of Cannon Mountain, the distinctive beauty of New England's mountainous wilderness is as exhilarating to experience as it is impossible to forget. Lakes spill from mountain gorges into frigid streams that work their way through pine-needled forest floors and over lichen-covered boulders, providing water, food, or habitation to the white-tailed deer, the porcupines and moose, the rabbits, squirrels, raccoons, bobcats, beavers, a variety of fish and many kinds of birds that inhabit New England's wooded hills and mountains.

From Maine's rocky cliffs and jagged inlets to Connecticut's beaches of sand and gravel, New England's coastline reveals the action of the retreating glacier, as shorelines were scraped and sculpted, rocks ground into sand or fragments, and collections of glacial till deposited to form such moraines as Cape Cod, Nantucket, Martha's Vineyard and Block Island. Residents and visitors alike enjoy all the New England seacoast has to offer: deep-sea fishing and whale-watching, clambake feasts and sunning on the beaches, strolling through sand dunes covered with beach grass and wildflowers, or watching the fog roll into a sleepy harbor.

The coastline's towns and cities—New Haven, Newport, Providence, Provincetown, Boston, Portsmouth and Portland, to name a few—are as diverse as they are appealing in their own particular ways. But apart from the wilderness, coastline, and cities, there is the world that is New England's essence: the everyday towns, the farmland counties and working communities that harbor a distinct breed of people. New Englanders combine the idealism of America's founding fathers and those immigrants who came in search of a better world with the shrewdness and realism that comes of living close to the land. This is a unique people, whose heritage lies closest to America's roots. For New England is more than a history or a geography: it is a spirit and a way of living.

Barbara Paulding Thrasher

RURAL NEW ENGLAND

The mossy stone walls in many of New England's woodlands testify to the region's past as a story of the struggle between man and nature. Although New England's earliest settlements were along its coast, trappers, traders, farmers and adventurers explored and settled inland areas in the early eighteenth century. Land was cleared as homesteads, farms, winding roads and villages became a part of the New England landscape. Western Massachusetts and northwestern Connecticut supported dairy farms and hayfields; in the following centuries the region would also become attractive for its colleges and the respite its serenity would offer to nearby city dwellers. Connecticut harbored institutions of commerce and industry as well as tobacco farms in the North, timber and agriculture. The smallest New England state, Rhode Island, would also become the most densely populated. Dairy farming, logging and later, tourism, would shape the face of rural Vermont, a state whose human population finally surpassed that of cows in 1965. Crisscrossed by logging trails and rushing rivers, New Hampshire's countryside supported farms as well as the occasional textile mill, but as in much of New England, nature would reclaim land as the sandy, rocky soil dissuaded many a would-be farmer. Although larger than the other New England states combined, Maine is the least populous. Potato farming as well as the timber and paper industries have made their slight marks on Maine's vast wilderness.

The architecture of rural New England is the best-known and best-loved in the country. It is the white, columned Georgian houses of Deerfield, Massachusetts, clapboarded capes with rose-covered trellises, Federal-style houses with balustrades and arching fanlights over their doorways, white church steeples rising above the villages. With its rich heritage, New England also bears the legacy of the Shakers, whose simple philosophy is reflected in their crafts and design.

Rural New England is square dances, auctions and country fairs as well, but its spirit is embodied in its seasons. Springtime finds crocuses pushing their way up through a snowy ground, people tapping trees for their annual maple sugar supply, impatient horses stamping in muddy fields, and trees swathed in a green haze as the buds begin to swell. In summer New England's coastline and many lakes offer respite from the heat, as the buzz of the cicada hangs in the hazy air, giving way to a chorus of crickets at night. Autumn brings the most visitors to New England, those intent on witnessing the vibrant colors of fall foliage engulf the mountains, hills and valleys. Pumpkins are harvested, and brilliant stars punctuate the chilly evening sky. Winter etches the houses' windows with frosty designs and blankets everything in snow. Winter, the season closest to New England's core, is the season that inspired Robert Frost to stop by the woods on a snowy evening to listen to 'the sweep of easy wind and downy flake.'

15 Maples in fall color frame a pristine church at Cornwall Bridge, Connecticut.

16/17 Waterville, Vermont, with its population of 470, nestles in a wooded valley.

18 Late winter and early spring, when the sap starts to flow, is the time for maple sugaring in New Hampshire.

19 A chilly snow-covered scene in Wardsboro, Vermont.

20/21 A view across the Old North Bridge in Concord, Massachusetts. The Minuteman Statue by Daniel Chester French, on the far side of the river, commemorates the Battle of Concord at the beginning of the American Revolution.

22 Old buildings at twilight are reflected in the West River at Londonderry, Vermont.

23 The blossoming of apple trees and dandelions in springtime gives new life to an old farm after a cold winter in Lempster, New Hampshire.

24/25 The stirrings of spring along a pastoral road in Hollis, New Hampshire.

26 *The Grist Mill at the Wayside Inn in Sudbury, Massachusetts.*

27 *The Green Bank Hollow covered bridge in South Danville, Vermont, spans Joe's Brook.*

28/29 *The Old Manse in Concord, Massachusetts, home of Reverend William Emerson, grandfather of Ralph Waldo Emerson. Here Nathaniel Hawthorne wrote* Mosses from an Old Manse.

30 *The House of Seven Gables in Salem,*
Massachusetts, built in 1668, was made famous
by Hawthorne's novel of the same name.

31 Historic Monroe Tavern, built in 1695, in Lexington, Massachusetts, faces the green where the Revolutionary War began.

32 A meadow nestled in the White Mountains of New Hampshire is ringed with brilliant birch and maple trees, accentuated by evergreens.

33 The maple trees along a country road near South Peacham, Vermont, become colorful sentinels in October.

34/35 Dramatic contrasts of light and dark highlight a fall morning in the village of Waits River in Vermont.

THE COASTLINE

The Northeast seacoast is one of New England's main attractions. Many visitors equate the entire region with images of the coast, although Vermont has no seacoast at all, and New Hampshire has very little. The pervasive local color of New England's coastline exudes a distinctive character that cannot be found anywhere else in the world.

New England's seacoast was shaped millennia ago by the advance and retreat of a vast glacier. The resulting sandy, rocky soil along much of the coast supports only hardy and adaptable plant life. Pitch pine and scrub oak on Cape Cod and the islands are among the few trees that can withstand the conditions; these gnarled and stunted individuals coexist with wild rose, blueberry bushes, holly and stretches of beach grass. The moors of Nantucket and Block Island, once used for grazing sheep, lack any trees. Their sandy valleys and rolling hills of heath, juniper and bayberry harbor a variety of songbirds, hawks, pheasants and even deer.

Much of the coastline, from Maine to Connecticut, is occupied by an assortment of houses, resorts, harbors and active or former fishing villages. Boston's North Shore features the lovely old towns of Rockport, Marblehead and Gloucester, which typify the region with their narrow streets, unique architecture and welcoming piers. The sandy beaches of southern New England give way to a more rugged coastline in the north. Maine's granite bluffs and rugged inlets, topped with an occasional lighthouse, present their own kind of storm-lashed beauty. Lobstering and deep-sea fishing supply many a living, and Maine's coastal wilderness and remote islands are one of New England's most precious features.

The coast of New England is wind-swept beach grass rippling over sand dunes, colorful buoys bobbing in a dark blue ocean, fishing boats cutting through the dawn mist, the smell of suntan lotion and the cries of seagulls wafting over a beach of languid sunbathers, summer cottages with screen doors that never quite close, local entrepeneurs selling salt-water taffy or fresh produce, and the smell of ocean spray as it dashes against a rocky cliff.

37 Off Mount Desert Island, a fishing boat plies the waters of the Gulf of Maine.

38/39 A quiet evening reflection at Kennebunk in Maine's southernmost region, York County.

40 A vacationing family sunbathing on one of the many pleasant beaches of Nantucket Island in Massachusetts.

41 Friends wheel their way home along York Beach in Maine.

42 Wildflowers and beach grass nestle in the rocks on Maine's wind-swept Monhegan Island. The house of Jamie Wyeth can be seen in the background.

43 After a day of fishing, friends relax on the rocks along Greenwich Harbor in Connecticut. The southernmost town of the state, Greenwich calls itself the 'Gateway to New England.'

44/45 Pleasure boats in the peaceful waters of the harbor at Southport, Connecticut.

46/47 The harbor at Wickford, Rhode Island, becomes a study in shadow as the fog rolls in. Water laps the dock pilings as the muffled blast of a foghorn floats through the salty air.

48 Fishing boats line the docks of Provincetown Harbor at the tip of Cape Cod, Massachusetts.

49 A sea of yellow-green beach grass surrounds an old life-saving station at Race Point Beach, in the Province Lands Area of Cape Cod National Seashore.

50/51 A winter scene in the lovely town of Rockport on the North Shore of Massachusetts.

52 Lobstermen take a break during a busy day
in Corea, Maine.

53 Buoys and flowers create a seaside ambience
in Groton Point, Connecticut.

54/55 Sunset colors the harbor at Watch Hill,
Rhode Island.

56 The appeal of Martha's Vineyard is typified in
the unkempt beauty of this house and grounds.

57 Oldest of the Cape Cod mills, the windmill of
Eastham, Massachusetts, speaks of the rural past.

WILDERNESS

Nature's first green is gold,
Her hardest hue to hold.
Her early leaf's a flower
But only so an hour.

—Robert Frost

New England's seasons seem to change as quickly as her weather, except of course for winter, which holds sway even into April. When the sap begins to flow in the trees, and migratory birds return to establish territories and build nests, the wilderness of New England begins to take on a hospitable hue. By mid-summer meadows are filled with Queen Anne's lace and bursting milkweed pods and maple trees boast leaves the size of your hand.

Although New England's pioneers cleared land for settlements, farms and roads and stripped forests for timber, much of the region's native wilderness has been set aside and given government protection. New England's wilderness can be the woods behind your house, as many know whose rhododendrons are nibbled by deer or whose trash cans are sifted through by raccoons, or it can be Maine's untamed Baxter State Park or New Hampshire's beautiful Franconia Notch State Park. From bogs, with their characteristic wild cranberries, sphagnum mosses and leatherleaf, to the treeless peak of Mount Washington in the Presidential Range with its array of alpine wildflowers and tundra vegetation, New England's wilderness is as captivating as it diverse. Woodlands of poplar, fir, spruce, cedar, maple, beech, ash, oak, hemlock and cherry harbor white-tailed deer, red squirrels, beavers, snowshoe hares, rabbits and larger animals in the North, such as moose and the eastern coyote, which migrated here in the 1960s. The woodland floor is a fascinating world of old tree trunks, mossy stumps, fern patches, an occasional jack-in-the-pulpit, and huge granite boulders bequeathed by a glacier.

Mountain contours and their foothills shape much of New England, folding into deep gorges and valleys laced with streams nourished by lakes. The lakes offer only a few of the many enjoyments to man—fishing, boating and swimming—that the region has to offer. The best way to appreciate the wilderness is by experiencing it firsthand—canoeing through Maine's unspoiled waterways, rafting through white water, skiing, berrying, hiking, camping or birdwatching. The face of New England's wilderness is as fleeting as a turquoise dragonfly hovering among the cat-o'nine-tails, as changing as the moon rising over a wintry landscape, and as ever-lasting as the granite outcrop of a Maine mountaintop.

59 The waning sunset casts a twilight glow over
a lake in Baxter State Park, Maine.

60 Mist shrouds the Concord River in Concord,
Massachusetts.

61 The moon rises over a wintry landscape in
Goshen, Vermont.

62/63 A pair of young moose graze along a lake in Limestone, Maine.

64 *Two ski instructors top a ridge at Sugarbush, one of Vermont's many challenging ski resorts.*

65 White-water rafting in the turbulent west branch
of the Penobscot River in Maine.

66 *Blueberries ripen in the sandy forests along the Massachusetts coast.*

67 *Water rushes through rocks in the Hancock branch of the White River in Vermont's Green Mountain National Forest.*

68/69 *Afternoon light enhances the brilliant colors of an autumnal scene in Maine's Baxter State Park.*

70/71 A walking path along the ridge in New Hampshire's beautiful Franconia Notch.

72 Red maples and balsam fir line a bank of the Swift River in New Hampshire.

73 Water cascades from a mountain pool in New Hampshire's White Mountains National Forest.

74/75 Trees are etched in frost on Mount Mansfield in Vermont.

76 Mountains encircle Echo Lake in New Hampshire's Franconia Notch.

77 Birchs and autumn foliage give way to Mount Washington in the distance, viewed from Conway, New Hampshire.

78/79 Daffodils poke through a forest floor in East Hampton, Connecticut. The old stone wall indicates that this was once farmland.

BOSTON

Because of its small size and its colorful neighborhoods, Boston is not a city that overwhelms. Considered 'the hub' or 'the Athens of America' by many native Bostonians, Boston was for a long time New England's center of industry, commerce and culture. Founded in 1630 by a group of Puritans who had first landed at Salem, Boston's original hilly landscape was later levelled off to fill in the many swampy, low-lying areas. As Boston's usable land area expanded, so did her maritime trade and fishing industry, nurtured by a perfect natural harbor. When the British tightened their hold on their wayward colony, escalating tensions led to the Boston Massacre of 1770, and the legendary Boston Tea Party three years later, as the city became a focus for Revolutionary activity. Today Boston's Freedom Trail brings visitors to the city's major colonial and revolutionary landmarks.

With its growing wealth and population, America's oldest city became a mecca for American intellectualism, attracting writers, publishers and establishing over time such grand cultural institutions as the Museum of Fine Arts, the Boston Symphony Orchestra, and an amazing number of colleges and universities—of which about 150 can be found today in the metropolitan area. Boston's sister city across the Charles River, Cambridge, harbors America's oldest institution of higher learning, Harvard University, as well as the innovative MIT. Boston boasts another 'first' as well in Boston Common, America's oldest park. Sold to the city in 1634 by the city's earliest English settler, Reverend William Blaxton, the 45-acre park was used to pasture livestock, to publicly punish Quakers, thieves and others deemed offensive, to station Redcoats and to allow leisurely repose in the midst of urban hustle and bustle.

Although Boston flourished after the Revolution, the character of the city changed with the mid-nineteenth century waves of immigration. The Irish arrived in droves during and after the potato famine, and although they provided much of the raw labor needed by the growing city, their culture clashed with that of the Boston Brahmins. Other immigrants began arriving as well, coinciding with the beginning of the city's decline as industry moved south, lured by cheaper labor.

Today's Boston is a growing and revitalized city, a charming integration of traditional and modern. A center for the high technology industry, Boston is also an amalgamation of distinctive neighborhoods. Boston's colorful North End, now Italian, harbors Fanueil Hall with its lively shops and restaurants. Much of the city's 40-mile-long waterfront has been renovated, and Boston's meandering streets wind past the cobblestoned, gas-lit Beacon Hill, the fashionable houses of Back Bay, the upbeat shopping areas off Boylston and Newbury Streets, the posh marble Copley Place complex, and the lovely Charles River.

With roughly one half of Massachusetts' population residing in this city, Boston is certainly the hub of the state. Offering the first symphony, the first baseball game, the first opera or theatrical production to New Englanders from all six states, Boston is a special place indeed. The many-faceted city combines innovation and growth with a nation's past in its lovely buildings and its adaptable inhabitants.

81 A view of Boston from the water reveals the skyline's two most distinctive landmarks: the John Hancock building (right) and the Prudential Center (left).

82/83 Yachts crowd a Cambridge dock on the Charles River on an October afternoon, with the Boston skyline in the distance.

84/85 A picturesque view of the Massachusetts State Capitol Building in the snow.

86 All varieties of freshly cut flowers are available
at this makeshift market.

87 A vendor sells newpapers on a sidewalk along
the Boston Common.

88/89 A view of Boston, glimpsed from the air, reveals the buildings of downtown, which give way to the greenery of Boston Common, then the row of Back Bay's brownstones facing the Charles River, across which lies Cambridge.

90 Buildings crowd Boston's waterfront, rimmed
by a busy expressway.

91 A view down Boston's historic Beacon Street.

92 and 93 Boston's Fanueil Hall, originally a marketplace and meeting hall built in 1742, was recently restored and now houses a variety of restaurants and shops.

94 Relaxing around the sculpted fountain in
Boston Common.

95 The reflection of the Romanesque Trinity
Church in the mirrors of the John Hancock
building shows how old and new, historic and
modern, coexist in Boston.

96 Pleasure-boating on the Charles is one of the
summer's great treats in Cambridge.

97 A swanboat glides past willow trees in the
Boston Public Gardens.

98 The USS Constitution, 'Old Ironsides,' now a
museum, was revolutionary in its day as one of
the world's most powerful frigates.

99 Pigeons perch on old grave markers in the
Old Granary Burying Ground in Boston.

100 A mounted policeman on patrol in Boston.

101 A view over the buildings of Harvard University in Cambridge toward the Charles River.

GLIMPSES

Although each state nurtures the qualities that make it unique and well known, New England will surprise you if you let it. Here the old co-exists with the new, and sophistication abides with rural simplicity. Yet for all its disparity, New England has one of the strongest senses of regional identity in the country. As a place with a long and significant past, New England attracts many visitors every year. But despite its increasingly fashionable reputation, New England is—and always will be—a homesewn garment. And despite the image of New England as a place to go to, for many people—and not just her natives—New England will always be a place to come home to.

New England can be explained and described in history and travel books, but glimpses of New England—images with textures, sounds and smells—evoke a stronger sense of place, even a feeling of kinship. The features that make up New England and endow it with so much spirit are often hidden behind an historic edifice or tucked among sand dunes fronting the beach. New England can be glimpsed in a sunrise over Providence, the city founded on religious tolerance, in the sounds of a marching band minutes before the parade reaches you, in the long tail of a Morgan horse swishing away flies on a summer afternoon, in the smells of the sea permeating a harbor, and in the warmth of a hearth on a winter night.

103 Fog enshrouds the docks of coastal Maine where a lone seagull perches atop a post.

104/105 Harvested pumpkins on a Rhode Island farm summon up the spirit of autumn in New England.

106 Live lobsters and freshly dug clams are ready
to be placed over a pile of steaming seaweed for
a typical New England clambake in Connecticut.

107 A Maine family watches a parade undeterred
by the rain.

108/109 A snowy farmyard view in East Montpelier,
Vermont.

110/111 Reflections and afternoon light enhance
a Providence, Rhode Island skyline.

112 *The Fourth of July parade in Bristol, Rhode Island.*

113 *A detail of the restored ring-twister in Slater Mill. Operations began in 1791 in this cotton-spinning plant, which was America's first successful full-time factory.*

114/115 *A skilled boatmaker at his craft in Bath, Maine.*

116 A native of Martha's Vineyard, Massachusetts, passes an idle afternoon rocking on the post office porch.

117 A great Maine face at the Fourth of July parade in Bar Harbor.

118/119 A Morgan mare and her foal. The roots of this sturdy, all-purpose horse trace back to eighteenth-century Vermont.

120 The shadow of a student studying at Brown
University in Rhode Island.

121 A view of the Yale University campus in New
Haven in the late spring.

THEY THAT GO
DOWN TO THE SEA
IN SHIPS
▲   ▲   ▲
1623 — 1923

122 *The Fishermen's Memorial in Gloucester, Massachusetts, faces out over the seawall.*

123 *A cloud-strewn sky frames the Rockland Breakwater in Maine.*

124/125 *A serene sunset over the water at West Harpswell, Maine.*